A LITTLE
IRISH
QUOTATIONS

COMPILED BY SEAN McMAHON
ILLUSTRATED BY COLIN DAVIDSON

Appletree Press

First published by
The Appletree Press Ltd
19–21 Alfred Street
Belfast BT2 8DL
1994

A catalogue record for this book is available from the
British Library

ISBN 0 86281 480 4

Printed in the EU

9 8 7 6 5 4 3 2 1

Contents

OUT OF IRELAND HAVE I COME

This [the Irish] is a filthy people, wallowing in vice. Of all peoples it is the least instructed in the rudiments of the faith.

Giraldus Cambrensis *c.1147–c.1223*
Topographica Hiberniae

❧

She is of a gentle nature. If the anger of heaven be against her she will not bluster or storme, but she will weep many days together.

Justice Luke Gerson *fl. 1620*
Ireland Delineated

❧

Fair LIBERTY was all his cry.

Jonathan Swift *1667–1745*
Verses on the Death of Dr Swift

❧

He gave the little wealth he had
To found a house for fools and mad:
And show'd by one satiric touch,
No nation wanted it so much.

Jonathan Swift
Verses on the Death of Dr Swift

Erin, the tear and the smile in thine eyes
Blend like the rainbow that hangs in thy skies.

Thomas Moore *1779–1852*
Erin the Tear

❧

Rich and rare were the gems she wore,
And a bright gold ring on her wand she bore;
But oh! her beauty was far beyond
Her sparkling gems and snow-white wand.

Thomas Moore
Rich and Rare

❧

The harp that once thro' Tara's halls,
The soul of Music shed,
Now hangs as mute on Tara's walls
As if that soul were fled.

Thomas Moore
The Harp That Once

❧

Ireland is a fruitful mother of genius, but a barren nurse.

John Boyle O'Reilly *1844–90*
Watchwords

Think where man's glory most begins and ends,
And say my glory was I had such friends.

W B Yeats *1865–1939*
The Municipal Gallery Revisited

❧

Out of Ireland have we come,
Great hatred, little room,
Maimed us from the start.
I carry from my mother's womb
A fanatic heart.

W B Yeats
Remorse for Intemperate Speech

Then let the Orange Lily be
Thy badge my patriot brother—
The everlasting Green for me;
And—we for one another.

John de Jean Frazer *1809–52*
Song for July 12, 1843

❧

Subtleman: And how do you intend to live?
Teague: By eating, dear joy, when I can get it; and by sleeping
when I can get none:
'tish the fashion of Ireland.

George Farquhar *1677–1707*
The Twin-Rivals

❧

For the great Gaels of Ireland
Are the men that God made man,
For all their wars are merry
And all their songs are sad.

G K Chesterton *1874–1936*
Ballad of the White Horse

O Ireland, isn't it grand you look—
Like a bride in her rich adornin'?
And with all the pent-up love of my heart
I bid you the top of the mornin'!

John Locke *1847–89*
The Exile's Return

And Ireland long a province be
A Nation once again!

Thomas Davis *1814–45*
A Nation Once Again

In Ireland the inevitable never happens and the unexpected constantly occurs.

Sir John Pentland Mahaffy *1839–1919*

❧

Come back again—Come back to us, sometime—won't you? Oh the heart-cry of the Gael! It is heard so often in Eirinn that the very echoes of the land have learned it.

William Bulfin *1864–1910*
Rambles in Eirinn

❧

I have been accustomed to understand by Ireland, not merely a country possessing certain geographical features but a country inhabited by a certain people whom I know.

Isaac Butt *1813–79*
The Irish People and the Irish Land

❧

Ireland is a small but insuppressible island half an hour nearer the sunset than Great Britain.

Thomas Kettle *1880–1916*
On Crossing the Irish Sea

What I especially like about Englishmen is that after they have called you a thief and a liar and patted you on the back for being so charming in spite of it, they look honestly depressed if you fail to see that they are paying you a handsome compliment.

Robert Lynd *1879–1949*
Irish and English

৯৯

This lovely land that always sent
Her writers and artists to banishment
And in the spirit of Irish fun
Betrayed her own leaders, one by one.

James Joyce *1882–1941*
Gas from a Burner

৯৯

I will not serve that in which I no longer believe, whether it call itself my home, my fatherland, or my church: and I will try to express myself in some mode of life or art as freely as I can and as wholly as I can, using for my defence the only arms I allow myself to use—silence, exile and cunning.

James Joyce
A Portrait of the Artist as a Young Man

Do you know what Ireland is? asked Stephen with cold venom.
Ireland is the old sow that eats her farrow.

James Joyce
A Portrait of the Artist as a Young Man

Amazed the gazing rustics rang'd around,
And still they gaz'd and still the wonder grew,
That one small head could carry all he knew.

Oliver Goldsmith *1730–74*
The Deserted Village

Whenever I wanted to know what the Irish people wanted, I had only to examine my own heart and it told me straight off what the Irish people wanted.

Eamon De Valera *1882–1975*
Dáil Éireann, 6 January 1922

In Ireland a policeman's lot is a supremely happy one. God smiles, the priest beams, and the novelist groans.

Sean ÓFaoláin *1900–92*
The Dilemma of Irish Letters

. . . mad Ireland hurt you into poetry.
Now Ireland has her madness and her weather still,
For poetry makes nothing happen.

W H Auden *1907–1973*
In Memory of WB Yeats

❦

Ireland's a door where the living collogue with the dead.

Francis MacManus *1909–65*
Praise God for Ireland

❦

Irishness is not primarily a question of birth or blood or language;
it is the condition of being involved in the Irish situation, and
usually of being mauled by it.

Conor Cruise O'Brien *b. 1917*
Irishness

❦

Dear Erin, how sweetly thy green bosom rises!
An emerald set in the ring of the sea.

John Philpot Curran *1750–1817*
Cushla Ma Chree

THE HUMOUR IS ON ME

❧

Being moderately taken...it sloweth age, it strengtheneth youth, it helpeth digestion, it cutteth flegme, it abandoneth melancholie, it relisheth the heart, it lighteneth the mind, it quickeneth the spirits . . .

Richard Stanihurst *1547–1618*
Aqua Vitae

❧

I wish either my father or mother, or indeed both of them, as they were in duty both equally bound to it, had minded what they were about when they begot me.

Laurence Sterne *1713–68*
Tristram Shandy

❧

Brian O'Linn and his wife and wife's mother,
They all crossed over the bridge together.
The bridge broke down and they all tumbled in—
'We'll go home by water', said Brian O'Linn.

Anonymous *18th Century*
Brian O'Linn

A circulating library in a town is an ever-green tree of diabolical knowledge! It blossoms through the year!

Richard Brinsley Sheridan *1759–1816*
The Rivals

She's as headstrong as an allegory on the banks of the Nile.

Richard Brinsley Sheridan *1759–1816*
The Rivals

Sir:
I am not so great a fool as you take me for. I have been bitten once by you, and I will never give you an opportunity of taking two bites of
A. Cherry

Andrew Cherry *1762–1812*
Letter to the manager of a Dublin theatre

In Glendalough lived a young saint,
In odour of sanctity dwelling,
An old-fashioned odour, which now
We seldom or never are smelling.

Samuel Lover *1797–1868*
St Kevin

Of priests we can offer a charming variety,
Far renowned for larnin' and piety;
Still I'd advance ye widout impropriety,
Father O'Flynn as the flower of them all.

A P Graves *1846–1931*
Father O'Flynn

ஐ

When money's tight and is hard to get
And your horse has also ran,
When all you have is a heap of debt—
A PINT OF PLAIN IS YOUR ONLY MAN.

Flann O'Brien *1911–66*
At Swim-Two-Birds

ஐ

The gross and net result of it is that people who spend most of
their natural lives riding iron bicycles over the rocky roadsteads of
this parish get their personalities mixed up with the personalities of
their bicycles as a result of the interchanges of the atoms of each of
them and you would be surprised at the number of people in these
parts who are nearly half people and half bicycles.

Flann O'Brien
The Third Policeman

An' as it blowed an' blowed, I often looked up at the sky an' assed meself the question—what is the stars, what is the stars?

Sean O'Casey *1880–1964*
Juno and the Paycock

It's only a little cold I have; there's nothing derogatory wrong with me.

Sean O'Casey
The Plough and the Stars

On Egypt's banks, contagious to the Nile
The Ould Pharaoh's daughter, she went to bathe in style.
She took her dip and she came unto the land
And to dry her royal pelt she ran along the strand.

Zozimus *1794–1846*
The Finding of Moses

⁊♣

O long life to the man who invinted potheen—
Sure the Pope ought to make him a martyr—
If myself was this moment Victoria, our Queen,
I'd drink nothing but whiskey and wather.

Zozimus
In Praise of Potheen

⁊♣

Saint Patrick was a gintleman, he came of decent people,
In Dublin town he built a church, and upon't put a steeple;
His father was an O'Callaghan, his mother was a Brady,
His aunt was an O'Shaughnessy, his uncle was a Grady.

Zozimus
Saint Patrick Was a Gintleman

Anyone acquainted with Ireland knows that the morning of St Patrick's Day consists of the night of the 17th of March, flavoured strongly with the morning of the 18th.

'Ballyhooley' (Robert J Martin)
St Patrick's Day in the Morning

❧

You've heard o' Julius Caesar an' the great Napoleon too,
And how the Cork Militia bate the Turks at Waterloo,
But there's a page of history that, as yet, remains uncut,
An' that's the Martial story o' the Shlathery's Mounted Fut.

Percy French *1854–1920*
Slattery's Mounted Fut

❧

All I ever seemed to get was the kind of girl who had a special dispensation from Rome to wear the thickest part of her legs below the knee.

Hugh Leonard *b.1926*
Da

❧

My grandmother made dying her life's work.

Hugh Leonard
Home before Night

'More rain coming,' said Mr Knox, rising composedly; 'you'll have to put a goose down these chimneys some day soon, it's the only way to clean them.

Somerville & Ross (Edith Oenone Somerville *1858–1949 and* **Violet Martin** *1862–1915*)
Some Experiences of an Irish RM

&

Here's to the Pope in Killybuck, and may there be strife between Orange and Green as long as Alexander McCracken has a bad farm of land to sell.

Louis J Walsh *1880–1942*
The Pope in Killybuck

Here's to the maiden of bashful fifteen;
Here's to the widow of fifty;
Here's to the flaunting extravagant quean;
And here's to the housewife that's thrifty.

Richard Brinsley Sheridan *1759–1816*
The School for Scandal

Oh! hast thou forgotten this day we must part?
It may be for years and it may be for ever.

Julia Crawford *c.1799–c.1860*
Kathleen Mavourneen

I'm very lonely now, Mary,
For the poor make no new friends.

Lady Helen Selina Sheridan Blackwood Dufferin *1807–1867*
Lament of the Irish Emigrant

❧

But the heart that has truly loved, never forgets,
But as truly loves on to the close.

Thomas Moore *1779–1852*
Believe Me

❧

. . . there's nothing half so sweet in life
As love's young dream.'

Thomas Moore
Oh, The Days Are Gone

❧

My only books
Were Woman's looks,
And Folly's all they taught me.

Thomas Moore
The Time I've lost

She is far from the land where her young hero sleeps,
  And lovers around her are sighing;
But coldly she turns from their gaze, and weeps
  For her heart in his grave is lying.

Thomas Moore
She is Far from the Land

To love oneself is the beginning of a lifelong romance.

Oscar Wilde *1854–1900*
An Ideal Husband

❧

Well, the heart's a wonder; and, I'm thinking, there won't be our
like in Mayo, for gallant lovers, from this hour today.

J M Synge *1871–1909*
The Playboy of the Western World

❧

Oh, I'd rather live in poverty with little Mary Cassidy
Than Emperor without her be o'er Germany or Spain.

Francis Arthur Fahy *1854–1935*
Little Mary Cassidy

❧

When you are old and grey and full of sleep,
And nodding by the fire, take down this book,
And slowly read, and dream of the soft look
Your eyes had once and of their shadows deep.

W B Yeats *1865–1939*
When You Are Old

ON THE EDGE

She lays it on with a trowel.

William Congreve *1670–1729*
The Double Dealer

٭

Alack, he's gone the way of all flesh.

William Congreve
Squire Bickerstaff Detected

٭

The Irish are a fair people;—they never speak well of one another.

Samuel Johnson *1709–84*
Boswell, *Life of Johnson*

٭

It is the nature of all greatness not to be exact.

Edmund Burke *1729–97*
American Taxation

Too nice an inquisition should not be made into opinions that are dying away by themselves.

Edmund Burke
Letter to Samuel Span

❧

You should always except the present company.

John O'Keefe *1747–1833*
The London Hermit

❧

Happiness is no laughing matter.

Richard Whately, Archbishop of Dublin *1787–1863*
Apophthegms

❧

She's the sort of woman who lives for others—you can always tell the others by their hunted expression.

C S Lewis *1898–1963*
The Screwtape Letters

I have just read a long novel by Henry James. Much of it made me think of the priest condemned for a long space to confess nuns.

John Butler Yeats *1839–1922*

❧

It [the Turko-Grecian war, 1912–13] was like waiting for a train in Mullingar.

Stephen MacKenna *1872–1934*

❧

In those days the common people ideally separated the gentry of the country into three classes according to the relative degree of respect to which they considered it was entitled. They generally divided them thus: 1 Half-mounted gentlemen; 2 Gentlemen every inch of them; 3 Gentlemen to the backbone.

Sir Jonah Barrington *1760–1834*
Personal Sketches

❧

Last week I saw a woman flayed, and you will hardly believe how much it altered her person for the worse.

Jonathan Swift *1667–1745*
Digression on Madness

❧

The Carmelites will do their best to get him. He would be wasted with them—the boy ought to be a scholar, not a pulpit wind-bag.

Jeremiah 'Gerald' O'Donovan *1871–1942*
Father Ralph

❧

Anybody can be good in the country.

Oscar Wilde *1854–1900*
The Critic as Artist

෴

No woman should ever be quite accurate about her age. It looks so calculating.

Oscar Wilde
The Importance of Being Earnest

෴

I can resist everything except temptation.

Oscar Wilde
Lady Windermere's Fan

෴

To lose one parent, Mr Worthing, may be regarded as a misfortune; to lose both looks like carelessness.

Oscar Wilde
The Importance of Being Earnest

Work is the curse of the drinking classes.

Oscar Wilde
Lady Windermere's Fan

๕

Peel's smile was like the silver plate on a coffin.

Daniel O'Connell *1775–1848*

AS I ROVED OUT

In burgo Duno tumulo; tumulantur in uno
Brigida, Patricius, atque Columba Pius.
[In Down three saints one grave do fill
Brigid, Patrick and Colmcille.]

John De Courcy *d.1219*

Boswell: Is not the Giant's Causeway worth seeing?
Johnson: Worth seeing? Yes, but not worth going to see.

Samuel Johnson *1709–84*
Boswell, *Life of Johnson*

O stony grey soil of Monaghan
The laugh from my love you thieved.

Patrick Kavanagh *1904–67*
Stony Grey Soil

The bar-room was forgotten and all that concerned it, and the things he saw most clearly were the green hillside, and the bog-lake and the rushes about it, and the greater lake in the distance, and behind it the blue line of wandering hills.

George Moore *1852–1933*
Home Sickness

But – hark! – some voice like thunder spake:
The West's awake! the West's awake!

Thomas Davis *1814–45*
The West's Asleep

And tones that are tender and tones that are gruff
Are whispering over the sea,
'Come back, Paddy Reilly, to Ballyjamesduff,
Come home, Paddy Reilly, to me.'

Percy French *1854–1920*
Come Back, Paddy Reilly

❧

But if at those roses you ventured to sip,
The colour might all come away on your lip
So I'll wait for the wild rose that's waitin' for me—
Where the Mountains of Mourne sweep down to the sea.

Percy French
The Mountains of Mourne

❧

. . . my sentimental regard for Ireland does not include the capital.

George Bernard Shaw *1856–1950*
Immaturity

❧

Your first day in Dublin is always your worst.

John Berryman *1914–1972*
The Dream Songs

❧

Yes, the newspapers were right; snow was general all over Ireland. It was falling on every part of the dark central plain, on the treeless hills, falling softly upon the Bog of Allen and, farther westward, softly falling into the dark mutinous Shannon waves.

James Joyce *1882–1941*
The Dead

❧

riverrun, past Eve and Adam's, from swerve of shore to bend of bay, brings us by a circuitous vicus of recirculation back to Howth Castle and Environs.

James Joyce
Finnegans Wake

❧

'But in the lonely hush of eve
Weeping I grieve the silent bills.'
I heard the Poor Old Woman say
In Derry of the little hills.

Francis Ledwidge *1891–1917*
Lament for the Poets: 1916

Red brick in the suburbs, white horse on the wall,
Eyetalian marbles in the City Hall:
O stranger from England, why stand so aghast?
May the Lord in his mercy be kind to Belfast.

Maurice James Craig *b.1919*
Ballad to a Traditional Refrain

I take my stand by the Ulster names,
each clean hard name like a weathered stone;
Tyrella, Rostrevor, are flickering flames:
the names I mean are the Moy, Malone,
Strabane, Slieve Gullion and Portglenone.

John Hewitt *1907–87*
Ulster Names

In doggerel and stout let me honour this country
Though the air is so soft that it smudges the words.

Louis MacNeice *1907–63*
Western Landscape

Armagh: where two cathedrals sit upon opposing hills like the
horns of a dilemma.

Sam Hanna Bell *1909–90*
In Praise of Ulster

DEAR THOUGHTS

But with the actor it is different: we are born at the rise of the curtain and we die with its fall, and every night in the presence of our patrons we write our new creation, and every night it is blotted out forever; and of what use is it to say to audience or to critic, 'Ah but you should have seen me last Tuesday!'

Micheál mac Liammóir *1899–1978*
Hamlet in Elsinore

I shall not go to heaven when I die,
But if they will let me be
I think I'll take the road I use to know
That goes by Shere-na-garagh and the sea.

Helen Waddell *1889–1965*
I Shall not Go to Heaven

We are the music makers,
We are the dreamers of dreams.

Arthur O'Shaughnessy *1841–81*
Ode

❧

There is wishful thinking in Hell as well as on earth.

C S Lewis *1898–1963*
The Screwtape Letters

❧

Och! but I'm weary of mist and dark,
And roads where there's never a house or bush!

Padraic Colum *1881–1957*
An Old Woman of the Roads

There is a lake in every man's heart...and he listens to its monotonous whisper year by year until at last he ungirds.

George Moore *1852–1933*
The Lake

Yet each man kills the thing he loves.

Oscar Wilde *1854–1900*
The Ballad of Reading Gaol

The truth is rarely pure, and never simple.

Oscar Wilde
The Importance of Being Earnest

I have nothing to declare except my genius.

Oscar Wilde
At New York Customs House

I remember on one occasion when she [his mother] was asked to sing the English version of that touching melody 'The Red-haired Man's Wife', she replied, 'I will sing it for you; but the English words and the air are like a quarrelling man and wife; *the Irish melts into the tune* but the English doesn't.'

William Carleton *1794–1869*
Traits and Stories of the Irish Peasantry

But the age of chivalry is gone. That of the sophisters, economists and calculators has succeeded.

Edmund Burke *1729–97*
Reflections on the Revolution in France

Men thought it a region of sunshine and rest,
And they called it Hy-Brasail, the isle of the blest.

Gerald Griffin *1803–49*
Hy-Brasail

When lovely woman stoops to folly
And finds too late that men betray,
What charm can soothe her melancholy,
What art can wash her guilt away?

Oliver Goldsmith *1730–74*
The Vicar of Wakefield

ɞ

Honesty is the best policy; but he that is governed by that maxim
is not an honest man.

Richard Whately, Archbishop of Dublin *1787–1863*
Apophthegms

ɞ

Dear thoughts are in my mind
And my soul soars enchanted,
As I hear the sweet lark sing
In the clear air of the day.

Sir Samuel Ferguson *1810–86*
The Lark in the Clear Air

ɞ

It was like a miracle; but before our very eyes, and almost in the
drawing of a breath, the whole body crumbled into dust and
passed from our sight.

Abraham ('Bram') Stoker *1847–1912*
Dracula

Satire is a sort of glass wherein beholders do generally discover everyone's face but their own.

Jonathan Swift *1667–1745*
The Battle of the Books

Instead of dirt and poison we have rather chosen to fill our hives with honey and wax; thus furnishing mankind with the two noblest of things, which are sweetness and light.

Jonathan Swift
The Battle of the Books

He had been eight years upon a project for extracting sunbeams out of cucumbers, which were to be put into phials hermetically sealed, and let out to warm the air in raw inclement summers.

Jonathan Swift
Gulliver's Travels

And he gave it for his opinion, that whoever could make two ears of corn or two blades of grass to grow upon a spot of ground where only one grew before, would deserve better of mankind, and do more essential service to his country than the whole race of politicians put together.

Jonathan Swift

Gulliver's Travels

The intellect is forced to choose
Perfection of the life, or of the work.

W B Yeats *1865–1939*
The Choice

&

I see His blood upon the rose
And in the stars the glory of His eyes.

Joseph Mary Plunkett *1887–1916*
I See His Blood upon the Rose

The beauty of the world hath made me sad,
This beauty that will pass.

Patrick Pearse *1879–1916*
The Wayfarer

꧁

In a good play every speech should be as fully flavoured as a nut or apple.

J M Synge *1871–1909*
The Playboy of the Western World

꧁

Don't strike me. I killed my poor father, Tuesday was a week, for doing the like of that.

J M Synge
The Playboy of the Western World

꧁

It's the life of a young man to be going on the sea, and who would listen to an old woman with one thing and she saying it over.

J M Synge
Riders to the Sea

Acknowledgements

The publisher wishes to thank the following for permission to reproduce copyright material:

Faber and Faber Ltd for "In Memory of W.B. Yeats" by W.H. Auden; Maurice Craig for "Ballad To A Traditional Refrain"; Blackstaff Press for "Ulster Names" by John Hewitt (from *The Collected Poems of John Hewitt*, edited by Frank Ormsby); the Trustees of the Estate of Patrick Kavanagh, c/o Peter Fallon, Literary Agent, Loughcrew, Oldcastle, Co. Meath, Ireland, for "Stony Grey Soil" by Patrick Kavanagh; Hugh Leonard for the excerpts from *Home Before Night* and *Da*; HarperCollins Publishers Ltd for *The Screwtape Letters* by C.S. Lewis; Michael Williams, Executor of the Estate of the late Dr Hilton Edwards, for the quotation by Micheál mac Liammóir; Paddy MacManus for "Praise God For Ireland" by Francis McManus; Faber and Faber Ltd for "Western Landscape" by Louis MacNeice; Conor Cruise O'Brien for his quotation; HarperCollins Publishers Ltd for quotations from *At Swim-Two-Birds* and *The Third Policeman* by Flann O'Brien; Eileen O'Casey and Macmillan London Ltd for the quotations by Sean O'Casey; the Society of Authors on behalf of the Bernard Shaw Estate for the quotation from *Immaturity*; the Curtis Brown Group Ltd, London, for the quotation from *Some Experiences of an Irish RM* by Somerville and Ross; Felicitas Corrigan for "I Shall Not Go To Heaven" by Helen Waddell.

While every effort has been made to contact copyright holders, the publisher would welcome information on any oversight which may have occurred.